DAILY
CALM

DAILY CALM

365 DAYS OF SERENITY

CALM

Photos and Wisdom to Soothe Your Spirit

NATIONAL GEOGRAPHIC

WASHINGTON, D.C.

Published by the National Geographic Society

Grateful acknowledgment is made for permission to reprint the stanza for December 24 from *In Praise of the Unfinished: Selected Poems* by Julia Hartwig, translated by John Carpenter and Bogdana Carpenter, translation copyright © 2008 by John Carpenter and Bogdana Carpenter. Used by permission of Alfred A. Knopf, a division of Random House, Inc.

Library of Congress Cataloging-in-Publication Data
Daily calm : 365 days of serenity.
p cm
ISBN 978-1-4262-1169-0 (hardback)
1. Photography, Artistic. 2. Photography--Psychological aspects. 3. Meditations. I. National Geographic Society (U.S.)
TR655.D35 2013
770--dc23
2013014294

The National Geographic Society is one of the world's largest nonprofit scientific and educational organizations. Founded in 1888 to "increase and diffuse geographic knowledge," the Society's mission is to inspire people to care about the planet. It reaches more than 400 million people worldwide each month through its official journal, *National Geographic*, and other magazines; National Geographic Channel; television documentaries; music; radio; films; books; DVDs; maps; exhibitions; live events; school publishing programs; interactive media; and merchandise. National Geographic has funded more than 10,000 scientific research, conservation, and exploration projects and supports an education program promoting geographic literacy.

For more information, visit www.nationalgeographic.com.
National Geographic Society
1145 17th Street N.W.
Washington, D.C. 20036-4688 U.S.A.

For information about special discounts for bulk purchases,
please contact National Geographic Books Special Sales: ngspecsales@ngs.org

For rights or permissions inquiries, please contact National Geographic Books Subsidiary Rights: ngbookrights@ngs.org

Printed in China

14/PPS/2

JANUARY

TRANSITION

JANUARY 1

Everything will change. The only question
is growing up or decaying.

~ YOLANDE CORNELIA "NIKKI" GIOVANNI

And the day came when the risk to remain tight in the bud
was more painful than the risk it took to blossom.

— ANAÏS NIN

JANUARY 3

You cannot travel on the Path
before you have become
that Path itself.

~ BUDDHA

We must go ahead
and see for ourselves.

~ JACQUES COUSTEAU

*Life forms no logical
patterns. It is haphazard
and full of beauties—
which I try to catch
as they fly by, for who
knows whether any of
them will ever return?*

~ MARGOT FONTEYN

JANUARY 6

If there is no struggle,
there is no progress.

~ FREDERICK DOUGLASS

*Faith is taking the first step even when
you don't see the whole staircase.*

~ MARTIN LUTHER KING, JR.

*One doesn't discover new lands
without consenting to lose sight of
the shore for a very long time.*

~ ANDRÉ GIDE

JANUARY 9

*All change is a miracle to
contemplate, but it is a miracle
which is taking place every instant.*

~ HENRY DAVID THOREAU

To reach the port of heaven,
we must sail sometimes with the
wind and sometimes against it—
but we must sail, and not drift,
nor lie at anchor.

~ OLIVER WENDELL HOLMES, SR.

The more you move, the stronger you'll grow,
not like a tree that can be killed
if you uproot it.

~ HA JIN

Begin at once to live,
and count each separate day
as a separate life.

~ LUCIUS ANNAEUS SENECA

To change is to live . . .
to live is to change . . .
and not to change is to die.

~ Tennessee Williams

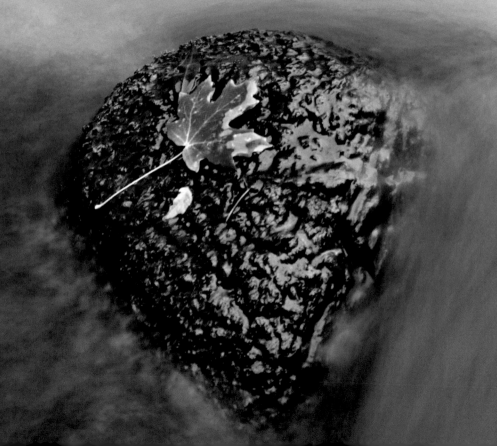

Dead my old fine hopes
And dry my dreaming, but oh . . .
Iris, blue each spring!

~ SHUSHIKI

Your hand opens and closes, opens and closes.
If it were always a fist or always stretched open,
you would be paralyzed.

~ RUMI

JANUARY 16

We are not yet what we shall be, but we are growing toward it, the process is not yet finished . . .

~ MARTIN LUTHER

*The joy of life comes from
our encounters with new experiences.
Hence there is no greater joy
than to have an endlessly changing horizon,
for each day to have a new
and different sun.*

~ CHRIS MCCANDLESS

*In three words, I can sum up
everything I've learned about life:
it goes on.*

~ ROBERT FROST

*As time passes we all get better at blazing
a trail through the thicket of advice.*

~ MARGOT BENNETT

*If the fish had stuck to its gills,
there would have been no movement
up to the land.*

~ CYNTHIA OZICK

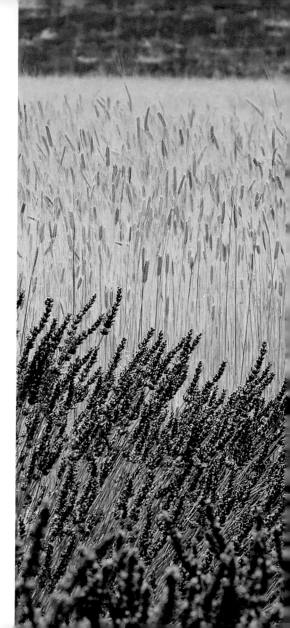

JANUARY 21

If we don't change,
we don't grow.
If we don't grow,
we are not really living.

~ GAIL SHEEHY

*There will come a time when
you believe everything is finished.
That will be the beginning.*

~ LOUIS L'AMOUR

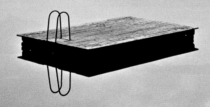

JANUARY 23

To improve is to change; to be perfect is to change often.

~ WINSTON CHURCHILL

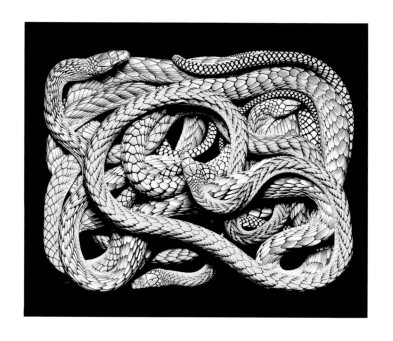

*The future is
of the same stuff as the present.*

~ SIMONE WEIL

An infinite question is often destroyed
by finite answers. To define everything is to
annihilate much that gives us laughter and joy.

~ MADELEINE L'ENGLE

*Every intersection in the road of life
is an opportunity to make a decision,
and at some I had only to listen.*

~ DUKE ELLINGTON

JANUARY 27

Our greatest glory consists
not in never falling,
but in rising every time we fall.

~ AMERICAN PROVERB

JANUARY 28

I am no longer what I was.
I will remain what I have become.

~ GABRIELLE "COCO" CHANEL

JANUARY 29

The moment of change
is the only poem.

~ Adrienne Rich

Disconnecting from change
does not recapture the past.
It loses the future.

~ KATHLEEN NORRIS

Our way is not soft grass,
it's a mountain path
with lots of rocks.
But it goes upwards,
forward, toward the sun.

~ RUTH WESTHEIMER

FEBRUARY

JOY

FEBRUARY 1

Grief can take care of itself;
but to get the full value of a joy
you must have somebody
to divide it with.

~ MARK TWAIN

Thousands of candles can be lighted from a single candle, and the life of the candle will not be shortened. Happiness never decreases by being shared.

~ BUDDHA

FEBRUARY 3

*A merry heart doeth good
like a medicine.*

~ PROVERBS 17:22

*Laughter is the sun which drives winter
from the human face.*

~ VICTOR HUGO

Peace is joy at rest
and joy is peace on its feet.

~ ANNE LAMOTT

He who bends to himself a Joy
Doth the winged life destroy;
But he who kisses the Joy as it flies
Lives in Eternity's sunrise.

~ WILLIAM BLAKE

FEBRUARY 7

We're so engaged in doing things to achieve purposes of outer value that we forget that the inner value— the rapture that is associated with being alive, is what it's all about.

~ JOSEPH CAMPBELL

How truly is a kind heart a fountain of gladness, making everything in its vicinity freshen into smiles.

~ WASHINGTON IRVING

FEBRUARY 9

*The essence of pleasure
is spontaneity.*

~ GERMAINE GREER

Against the assault of laughter nothing can stand.

~ MARK TWAIN

Kiss, n. A word invented by the poets
as a rhyme for "bliss."

~ AMBROSE BIERCE

The supreme happiness of life
is the conviction of being loved
for yourself, or, more correctly speaking,
loved in spite of yourself.

~ VICTOR HUGO

Mirth is like a flash of lightning,
that breaks through a gloom of clouds,
and glitters for a moment; cheerfulness keeps up a
kind of daylight in the mind, and fills it with
a steady and perpetual serenity.

~ JOSEPH ADDISON

FEBRUARY 14

Where there is joy
there is creation.

~ HINDU SCRIPTURE

Rapidly, merrily,
Life's sunny hours flit by,
Gratefully, cheerily,
Enjoy them as they fly!

~ CHARLOTTE BRONTË

Why not seize the pleasure at once?
—how often is happiness destroyed by
preparation, foolish preparation!

~ JANE AUSTEN

FEBRUARY 17

What's the earth with all its art,
verse, music worth—compared with
love, found, gained, and kept?

~ ROBERT BROWNING

FEBRUARY 18

Friendship improves happiness and abates misery,
by the doubling of our joy and the dividing of our grief.

~ MARCUS TULLIUS CICERO

Earth laughs in flowers . . .

~ RALPH WALDO EMERSON

To be in love is to touch things
with a lighter hand.

~ GWENDOLYN BROOKS

FEBRUARY 21

*. . . feel the stars and the infinite high
and clear above you. Then life seems
almost enchanted after all.*

~ VINCENT VAN GOGH

FEBRUARY 22

*Joy is prayer; joy is strength; joy
is love; joy is a net of love
by which you can catch souls.*

~ MOTHER TERESA

FEBRUARY 23

There is no pleasure in having nothing to do; the fun is in having lots to do—and not doing it.

~ MARY LITTLE

Most folks are about as happy as they make up their minds to be.

~ ABRAHAM LINCOLN

Too much of a good thing
can be wonderful.

~ MAE WEST

If you want to be happy, be.

~ LEO TOLSTOY

FEBRUARY 27

*One cannot divine nor forecast the conditions that
will make happiness; one only
stumbles upon them by chance, in a lucky hour,
at the world's end somewhere, and holds fast to
the days, as to fortune or fame.*

~ WILLA CATHER

FEBRUARY 28/29

*With mirth and laughter let
old wrinkles come.*

~ WILLIAM SHAKESPEARE

MARCH

EXPERIENCE

MARCH 1

*Slide the weight from your shoulders
and move forward. You are afraid
you might forget, but you never will.
You will forgive and remember.*

~ BARBARA KINGSOLVER

MARCH 2

*You won't win
until you learn how to lose.*

~ KAREEM ABDUL-JABBAR

Growth and self-transformation
cannot be delegated.

~ LEWIS MUMFORD

*Our strength is often composed
of the weakness we're damned
if we're going to show.*

~ MIGNON MCLAUGHLIN

MARCH 5

*What we lack is not so much
leisure to do as time to reflect
and time to feel.*

~ MARGARET MEAD

MARCH 6

*The easiest way to avoid
wrong notes is to never open
your mouth and sing.
What a mistake that would be.*

~ JOAN OLIVER GOLDSMITH

March 7

Time ripens all things.
No man is born wise.

~ Miguel de Cervantes Saavedra

MARCH 8

Every beginning
is only a sequel, after all,
and the book of events
is always open halfway through.

~ WISŁAWA SZYMBORSKA

We ought not to look back,
unless it is to derive useful lessons
from past errors.

~ GEORGE WASHINGTON

*Mistakes are part of the dues one pays
for living a full life.*

~ SOPHIA LOREN

MARCH 11

You can't move so fast that you try to change the mores faster than people can accept it. That doesn't mean that you do nothing, but it means that you do the things that need to be done according to priority.

~ ELEANOR ROOSEVELT

*The past, present, and future mingle
and pull us backward, forward,
or fix us in the present.
We are made up of layers,
cells, constellations.*

— ANAÏS NIN

MARCH 13

In youth we learn, in age we understand.

~ MARIE VON EBNER-ESCHENBACH

MARCH 14

You practice and you get better.
It's very simple.

~ PHILIP GLASS

To assign unanswered letters their proper weight, to free us from the expectations of others, to give us back to ourselves—there lies the great, singular power of self-respect.

~ JOAN DIDION

MARCH 16

*We know too much
and feel too little.*

~ BERTRAND RUSSELL

*Above all, be the heroine of your life,
not the victim.*

~ NORA EPHRON

Time is the substance from which I am made.
Time is a river that carries me along,
but I am the river; it is a tiger that devours
me, but I am the tiger; it is a fire that
consumes me, but I am the fire.

~ JORGE LUIS BORGES

Nothing ever becomes real
till it is experienced.

~ JOHN KEATS

The man who has lived most is not he who has numbered the most years, but he who has had the keenest sense of life.

~ JEAN-JACQUES ROUSSEAU

It is a mistake to regard age as a downhill
grade toward dissolution. The reverse is true.
As one grows older, one climbs
with surprising strides.

~ GEORGE SAND

*Adventure is something you
seek for pleasure, or even
for profit . . . but experience
is what really happens to you
in the long run; the truth that
finally overtakes you.*

~ KATHERINE ANNE PORTER

*Each day, and the living of it, has to be
a conscious creation in which discipline
and order are relieved with some
play and pure foolishness.*

~ MAY SARTON

*We need other human beings
in order to be human.*

~ DESMOND TUTU

MARCH 25

People are like bicycles.
They can keep their balance
only as long as they keep moving.

~ ALBERT EINSTEIN

*If facts are the seeds that later
produce knowledge or wisdom,
then the emotions and the impressions
of the senses are the fertile soil in which
the seeds must grow.*

~ RACHEL CARSON

MARCH 27

Education is when you read the fine print.
Experience is what you get if you don't.

~ PETE SEEGER

MARCH 28

*Try new recipes, learn
from your mistakes,
be fearless, and above all
have fun.*

~ JULIA CHILD

MARCH 29

In the Book of Life,
The answers aren't in the back.

~ CHARLES M. SCHULZ

MARCH 30

A man of genius makes no mistakes.
His errors are volitional
and are the portals of discovery.

~ JAMES JOYCE

To move, to breathe, to fly, to float
To gain all while you give,
To roam the roads of lands remote,
To travel is to live!

~ HANS CHRISTIAN ANDERSEN

APRIL

SIMPLICITY

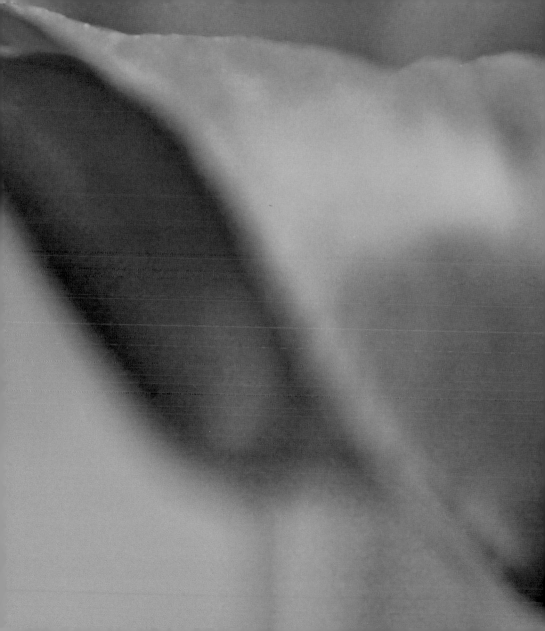

*It is the sweet, simple things of life
which are the real ones after all.*

~ LAURA INGALLS WILDER

*Don't eat anything your great-grandmother
wouldn't recognize as food.*

~ MICHAEL POLLAN

*To find the air and the water exhilarating;
to be refreshed by a morning walk or an evening saunter;
to be thrilled by the stars at night; to be elated over
a bird's nest, or over a wild flower in spring—
these are some of the rewards of the simple life.*

~ JOHN BURROUGHS

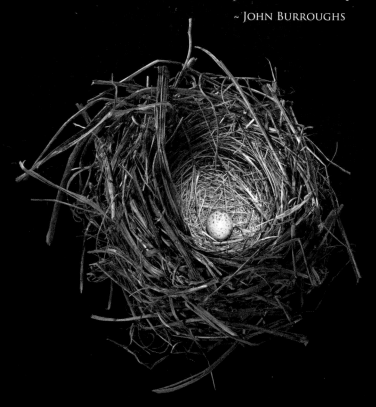

*The wisdom of life consists in the
elimination of non-essentials.*

~ LIN YUTANG

*The art of art, the glory of
expression and the sunshine
of the light of letters,
is simplicity.*

~ WALT WHITMAN

*Simplify the problem of life: distinguish
the necessary and the real. Probe the earth
to see where your main roots run.*

~ HENRY DAVID THOREAU

Everything deep is also simple.

~ ALBERT SCHWEITZER

Silence is more musical
than any song.

~ CHRISTINA ROSSETTI

*Most of the luxuries, and many of
the so-called comforts of life, are not
only not indispensable, but positive
hindrances to the elevation of mankind.*

~ Henry David Thoreau

APRIL 10

I adore simple pleasures.
They are the last refuge of the complex.

~ OSCAR WILDE

*Broadly speaking,
short words are best,
and the old words, when short,
are best of all.*

~ WINSTON CHURCHILL

Have nothing in your house that you do not know to be useful, or believe to be beautiful.

~ WILLIAM MORRIS

Making the simple complicated is commonplace; making the complicated simple, awesomely simple, that's creativity.

~ CHARLIE MINGUS

As I grew older, I realized that it was much better to insist on the genuine forms of nature, for simplicity is the greatest adornment of art.

~ ALBRECHT DÜRER

Be good, keep your feet dry, your eyes open,
your heart at peace . . .

~ THOMAS MERTON

Omit needless words.

~ WILLIAM STRUNK AND E. B. WHITE

APRIL 17

Joy in looking and comprehending
is nature's most beautiful gift.

~ ALBERT EINSTEIN

*To me a lush carpet of pine needles
or spongy grass is more welcome than
the most luxurious Persian rug.*

~ HELEN KELLER

APRIL.19

*Let things taste of
what they are.*

~ ALICE WATERS

Reduce the complexity of life by eliminating the needless wants of life, and the labors of life reduce themselves.

~Edwin Way Teale

*Simplicity is an exact medium
between too little and too much.*

~ SIR JOSHUA REYNOLDS

*Rain is grace; rain is the sky
condescending to the earth;
without rain, there would be no life.*

~ JOHN UPDIKE

APRIL 23

Very little is needed to
make a happy life.

~ MARCUS AURELIUS

The smell of good bread baking,
like the sound of lightly flowing water,
is indescribable in its evocation of
innocence and delight.

~ M. F. K. FISHER

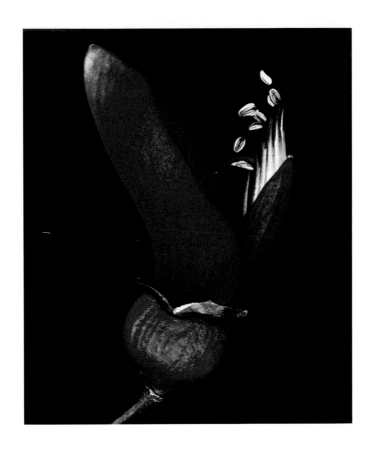

APRIL 25

Simplicity is the keynote
of all true elegance.

~ GABRIELLE "COCO" CHANEL

APRIL 26

Let silence take you
to the core of life.

~ RUMI

Learn to wish that everything
may happen as it does.

~ EPICTETUS

Believe that you have it,
and you have it.

~ LATIN PROVERB

APRIL 29

Do what you can, with what you've got,
where you are.

~ THEODORE ROOSEVELT

APRIL 30

*Sometimes the most
important thing in a whole
day is the rest we take
between two deep breaths.*

~ ETTY HILLESUM

MAY

MINDFULNESS

MAY 1

Look at your feet.
You are standing in the sky.
When we think of the sky,
we tend to look up, but the sky
actually begins at the earth . . .
We breathe it deep within us.

~ DIANE ACKERMAN

Go not abroad for happiness.
For see! it is a flower that blossoms by thy door.

~ MINOT J. SAVAGE

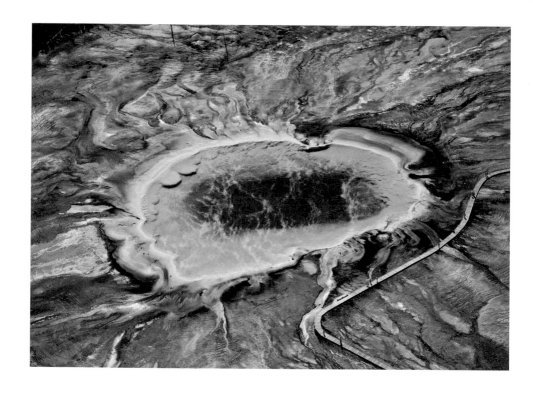

*It is only when we are aware of the earth and of
the earth as poetry that we truly live.*

~ HENRY BESTON

Being is sufficient. Being is All. The cheerful, sunny self you are missing will return, as it always does, but only being will bring it back.

~ ALICE WALKER

MAY 5

*Learning to live in the present moment
is part of the path of joy.*

~ SARAH BAN BREATHNACH

MAY 6

*Little by little, through patience
and repeated effort, the mind will
become stilled in the Self.*

~ HINDU SCRIPTURE

And forget not that the earth delights
to feel your bare feet and the winds long
to play with your hair.

~ KAHLIL GIBRAN

MAY 8

Only that day dawns to which we are awake.

~ HENRY DAVID THOREAU

*Happiness, not in another place
but this place . . . not for another
hour, but this hour.*

~ WALT WHITMAN

. . . those who do not observe the movements of their own minds must of necessity be unhappy.

~ MARCUS AURELIUS

Our true nature is not some deal that we have to live up to. It's who we are right now, and that's what we can make friends with and celebrate.

~ PEMA CHÖDRÖN

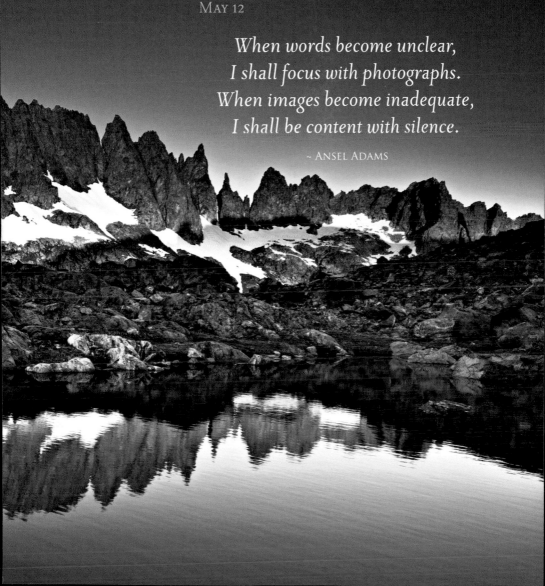

When words become unclear,
I shall focus with photographs.
When images become inadequate,
I shall be content with silence.

~ ANSEL ADAMS

MAY 13

The mind is its own place, and of itself can make a heaven of hell, a hell of heaven.

~ JOHN MILTON

Learn to be quiet enough to hear the sound of the genuine within yourself, so that you can hear it in other people.

~ MARIAN WRIGHT EDELMAN

MAY 15

Remember, remember,
this is now, and now, and now.
Live it, feel it; cling to it.

~ SYLVIA PLATH

Strange as it may seem today to say, the aim of life is to live, and to live means to be aware, joyously, drunkenly, serenely, divinely aware.

~ HENRY MILLER

The breeze of grace is always blowing on you,
but you have to unfurl your sails.

~ SRI RAMAKRISHNA

*The miracle is to walk on the green earth
in the present moment, to appreciate the peace
and beauty that are available now.*

~ THICH NHAT HANH

*Who looks outside, dreams;
who looks inside, awakes.*

~ CARL JUNG

Beauty and grace are performed
whether or not we will or sense them.
The least we can try to do is be there.

~ ANNIE DILLARD

You are a meeting place of gravitation and grace . . . You have something of the earth and something of the sky within you.

~ OSHO

MAY 22

Breathe-in experience,
breathe-out poetry.

~ MURIEL RUKEYSER

MAY 23

*Of many magics, one is watching
a beloved sleep: free of eyes and
awareness, you for a sweet moment
hold the heart of him.*

~ TRUMAN CAPOTE

MAY 24

It is more important
To see the simplicity,
To realize our true nature,
To cast off selfishness
And temper desire.

~ LAO-TZU

No longer forward or behind
I look in hope or fear;
But, grateful, take the good I find,
The best of now and here.

~ JOHN GREENLEAF WHITTIER

*You are only afraid if you are not
in harmony with yourself.*

~ HERMANN HESSE

Each situation—
nay, each moment—
is of infinite worth;
for each represents
a whole eternity.

~ JOHANN WOLFGANG VON GOETHE

MAY 28

. . . the more clearly we can focus
our attention on the wonders
and realities of the universe about us
the less taste we shall have
for the destruction of our race.

~ RACHEL CARSON

Let us not look back in anger,
nor forward in fear,
but around us in awareness.

~ JAMES THURBER

MAY 30

Listening to the birds can be a meditation
if you listen with awareness.

~ OSHO

MAY 31

You certainly usually find something,
if you look, but it is not always quite
the something you were after.

~ J. R. R. TOLKIEN

JUNE

COMPASSION

JUNE 1

One's life has value only so long as one attributes value to the lives of others by means of love, friendship, indignation, compassion.

~ SIMONE DE BEAUVOIR

*Kindness is the sunshine in
which virtue grows.*

~ ROBERT G. INGERSOLL

JUNE 3

*For those to whom much is
given, much is required.*

~ JOHN F. KENNEDY

JUNE 4

Constant kindness can accomplish much.
As the sun makes ice melt, kindness causes
misunderstanding, mistrust,
and hostility to evaporate.

~ ALBERT SCHWEITZER

What do we live for, if it is not to make life less difficult for each other?

~ GEORGE ELIOT

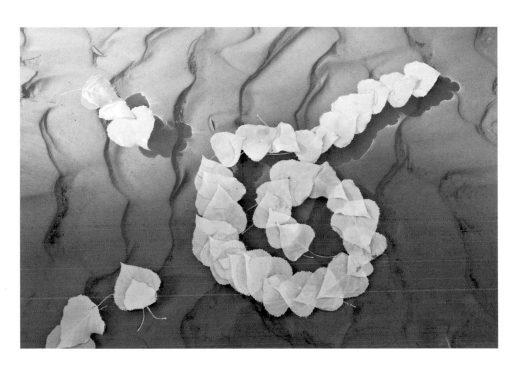

Compassion and tolerance
are not a sign of weakness,
but a sign of strength.

~ DALAI LAMA

Only if we understand, can we care.
Only if we care, will we help.
Only if we help, shall all be saved.

~ JANE GOODALL

There is no charm equal to
tenderness of heart.

~ JANE AUSTEN

With malice toward none;
with charity for all.

~ ABRAHAM LINCOLN

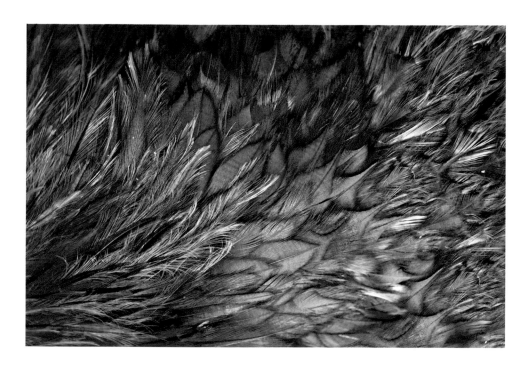

JUNE 10

The softest thing in the universe
overcomes the hardest.

~ LAO-TZU

*Sometimes people say unkind or
thoughtless things. When they do,
it is best to be a little hard of hearing.*

~ RUTH BADER GINSBURG

JUNE 12

He who sows courtesy
reaps friendship,
and he who plants
kindness gathers love.

~ PROVERB

*The more one judges,
the less one loves.*

~ HONORÉ DE BALZAC

JUNE 14

The highest virtue is to act without a sense of self. The highest kindness is to give without condition.

~ LAO-TZU

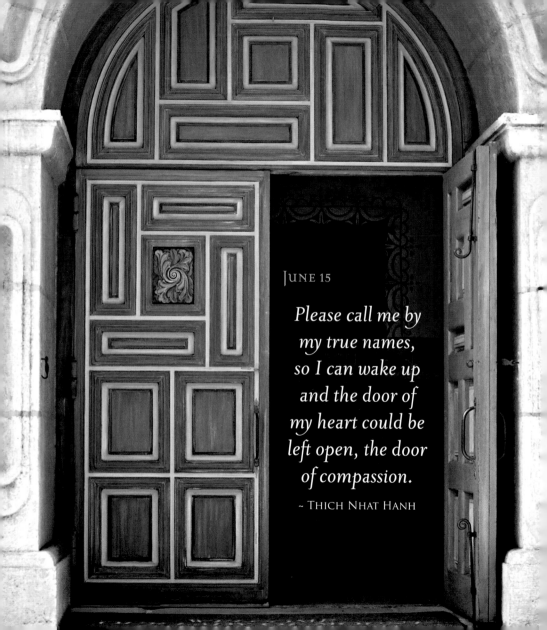

JUNE 15

*Please call me by
my true names,
so I can wake up
and the door of
my heart could be
left open, the door
of compassion.*

~ THICH NHAT HANH

Guard within yourself that treasure, kindness.
Know how to give without hesitation,
how to lose without regret,
how to acquire without meanness.

~ GEORGE SAND

*One kind word can warm
three winter months.*

~ JAPANESE PROVERB

Carry out a random act of kindness, with no expectations of reward, save that one day someone might do the same for you.

~ DIANA SPENCER, PRINCESS OF WALES

JUNE 19

*Grace, like water, flows from
a higher to a lower level.*

~ Śri Sathya Sai Baba

JUNE 20

*I always felt that the great high privilege,
relief and comfort of friendship was that
one had to explain nothing.*

~ KATHERINE MANSFIELD

When you are good to others,
you are best to yourself.

~ BENJAMIN FRANKLIN

Love doesn't just sit there, like a stone,
it has to be made, like bread;
re-made all the time, made new.

~ URSULA K. LE GUIN

*The giving of love is an
education in itself.*

~ ELEANOR ROOSEVELT

JUNE 24

From what we get, we can make a living;
what we give, however, makes a life.

~ ARTHUR ASHE

*Compassion will cure more
sins than condemnation.*

~ HENRY WARD BEECHER

The most important thing in anyone's life is to be giving something.

~ GINGER ROGERS

We can only learn to love by loving.

~ IRIS MURDOCH

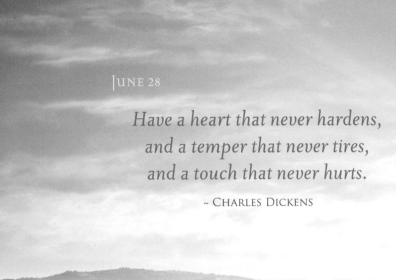

JUNE 28

Have a heart that never hardens,
and a temper that never tires,
and a touch that never hurts.

~ CHARLES DICKENS

JUNE 29

*Let your love be like the
misty rains, coming softly,
but flooding the river.*

~ MALAGASY PROVERB

The greatest good you can do for
another is not just to share your riches
but to reveal to him his own.

~ BENJAMIN DISRAELI

JULY

PERSPECTIVE

JULY 1

Revelation can be more perilous
than Revolution.

~ VLADIMIR NABOKOV

*We must understand ourselves
before we can respect ourselves.
We must respect ourselves before
we can win the respect of others.*

~ PEARL S. BUCK

JULY 3

*Art is a lie
that makes us realize truth.*

~ PABLO PICASSO

If the doors of perception were cleansed,
everything would appear to man
as it is, infinite.

~ WILLIAM BLAKE

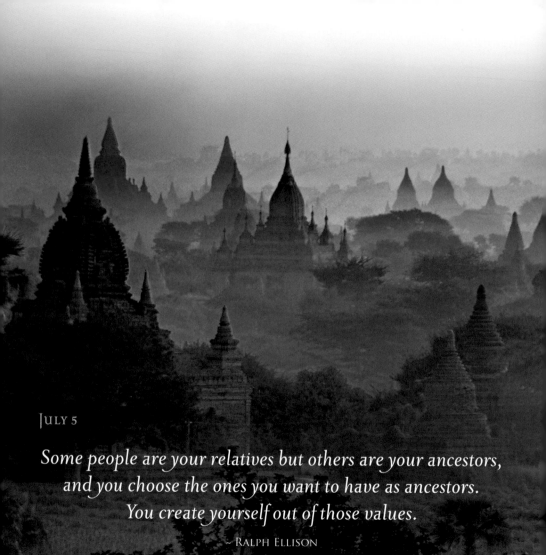

JULY 5

Some people are your relatives but others are your ancestors,
and you choose the ones you want to have as ancestors.
You create yourself out of those values.

~ RALPH ELLISON

I think we find happiness in retrospect.
We don't recognize it in the moment.

~ EVELYN CUNNINGHAM

JULY 7

For us believing physicists,
the distinction between past, present,
and future is only an illusion,
even if a stubborn one.

~ ALBERT EINSTEIN

Time has no divisions to mark its passage;
there is never a thunderstorm to announce the
beginning of a new year. Even when
a new century begins it is only we mortals
who ring bells and fire off pistols.

~ THOMAS MANN

*Imagination is the highest kite
that can fly.*

~ LAUREN BACALL

I want to stay as close to the edge as I can without going over. Out on the edge you can see all kinds of things you can't see from the center.

~ KURT VONNEGUT

*Anyone who keeps the ability to see beauty
never grows old.*

~ FRANZ KAFKA

*It is a narrow mind which
cannot look at a subject
from various points of view.*

~ GEORGE ELIOT

JULY 13

Days and months are travellers of eternity.
So are the years that pass by.

~ MATSUO BASHŌ

JULY 14

One generation passeth away,
and another generation cometh;
but the earth abideth forever.

~ ECCLESIASTES 1:4-5

We all live in suspense, from day to day,
from hour to hour; in other words,
we are the hero of our own story.

~ MARY MCCARTHY

The snake that cannot cast its skin
perishes. So too with those minds which
are prevented from changing their views:
they cease to be minds.

~ Friedrich Nietzsche

JULY 17

We are all in the gutter,
but some of us are looking
at the stars.

~ OSCAR WILDE

People from a planet without flowers
would think we must be mad with joy
the whole time to have such things about us.

~ IRIS MURDOCH

Better keep yourself clean and bright:
You are the window through which
you must see the world.

~ GEORGE BERNARD SHAW

*Some people could look at a mud-puddle
and see an ocean with ships.*

~ ZORA NEALE HURSTON

JULY 21

There is no such thing in anyone's life
as an unimportant day.

~ ALEXANDER WOOLLCOTT

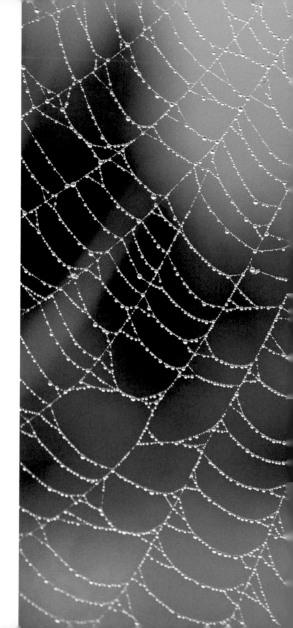

*Our thoughts,
our words, and deeds
are the threads of the
net which we throw
around ourselves.*

~ SWAMI VIVEKANANDA

A man who views the world the same at fifty as he did at twenty has wasted thirty years of his life.

~ MUHAMMAD ALI

The locus of the human mystery
is perception of this world.
From it proceeds every thought,
every art.

~ MARILYNNE ROBINSON

We shall not cease from exploration
And the end of all our exploring
Will be to arrive where we started
And know the place for the first time.

~ T. S. ELIOT

JULY 26

The voyage of discovery is not
in seeking new landscapes,
but in having new eyes.

~ MARCEL PROUST

*We come to love
not by finding a perfect person,
but by learning to see an imperfect
person perfectly.*

~ SAM KEEN

*To be seventy years young is sometimes
far more cheerful and hopeful
than to be forty years old.*

~ OLIVER WENDELL HOLMES, SR.

JULY 29

There is nothing noble about being superior to some other person. True nobility lies in being superior to your former self.

~ INDIAN PROVERB

JULY 30

It isn't the mountains ahead that wear you out,
it's the grain of sand in your shoe.

~ PROVERB

One can never read the same book twice.

~ EDMUND WILSON

AUGUST

PATIENCE

Drop by drop
is the pitcher filled.

~ BUDDHA

Patience is passion tamed.

~ LYMAN ABBOTT

Diamonds are nothing more than chunks of coal that stuck to their job.

~ MALCOLM FORBES

*Patience serves as a protection
against wrongs as clothes
do against cold.*

~ LEONARDO DA VINCI

August 5

*Nothing great is
produced suddenly.*

~ Epictetus

There are no stronger enemies
than patience and time.

~ LEO TOLSTOY

August 7

*An unhurried sense of time
is in itself a form of wealth.*

~ Bonnie Friedman

What wound did ever heal but by degrees?

~ William Shakespeare

Patience and diligence, like faith,
remove mountains.

~ WILLIAM PENN

AUGUST 10

*Patience, n. a minor form
of despair, disguised as a virtue.*

~ AMBROSE BIERCE

AUGUST 11

Someone is sitting in the shade today because
someone planted a tree a long time ago.

~ WARREN BUFFETT

AUGUST 12

*To drink in the spirit of a place you should
be not only alone but not hurried.*

~ GEORGE SANTAYANA

Experience has taught me this: that we undo ourselves by impatience. Misfortunes have their life and their limits, their sickness and their health.

~ MICHEL DE MONTAIGNE

AUGUST 14

Just when the caterpillar thought the world was over, it became a butterfly.

~ PROVERB

The thing that is really hard, and really amazing, is giving up on being perfect and beginning the work of becoming yourself.

~ ANNA QUINDLEN

Patience must be the charm
To heal me of my woe.

~ THOMAS WYATT

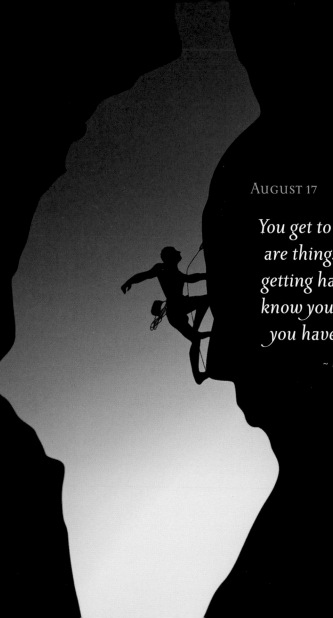

AUGUST 17

You get to the point when there are things you enjoy that start getting hard—that's when you know you're getting good, and you have to stick through it.

~ MICHELLE OBAMA

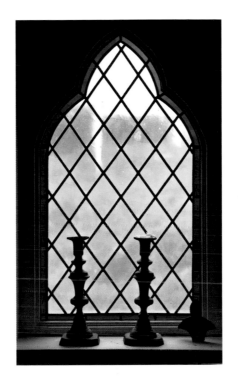

*All human wisdom is summed up
in two words—wait and hope.*

~ ALEXANDRE DUMAS

AUGUST 19

Who can wait quietly
while the mud settles?
Who can remain still
until the moment of
action?

~ LAO-TZU

Learn to labor and to wait.

~ HENRY WADSWORTH LONGFELLOW

Little strokes fell great oaks.

~ BENJAMIN FRANKLIN

The man who removes a mountain
begins by carrying away small stones.

~ CHINESE PROVERB

Trees slow of growth bear the best fruit.

~ MOLIÈRE

*With patience and time the
mulberry leaf becomes a silk gown.*

~ CHINESE PROVERB

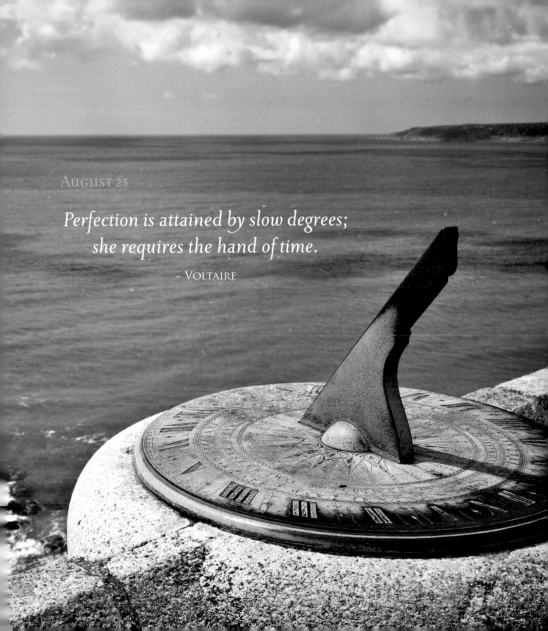

AUGUST 25

Perfection is attained by slow degrees;
she requires the hand of time.

~ VOLTAIRE

AUGUST 26

*Little drops of water
wear down big stones.*

~ RUSSIAN PROVERB

The best way out is always through.

~ ROBERT FROST

Rivers know this: there is no hurry.
We shall get there some day.

~ A. A. MILNE

AUGUST 29

When you come to the end of your rope, tie a knot and hang on.

~ AMERICAN PROVERB

*Genius is only a greater aptitude
for patience.*

~ Georges-Louis Leclerc de Buffon

*It's not that I'm so smart,
it's just that I stay with
problems longer.*

~ ALBERT EINSTEIN

SEPTEMBER

CONTENTMENT

SEPTEMBER 1

*What a lovely surprise
to discover how unlonely
being alone can be.*

~ ELLEN BURSTYN

Satisfaction is quietness of heart
under the course of destiny.

~ AL-HARITH AL-MUHASIBI

*Besides the noble art of getting things done,
there is a nobler art of leaving things undone.*

~ LIN YUTANG

SEPTEMBER 4

*The best way to pay for a
lovely moment is to enjoy it.*

~ RICHARD BACH

SEPTEMBER 5

When one is too old for love,
one finds great comfort
in good dinners.

~ ZORA NEALE HURSTON

SEPTEMBER 6

The one at peace sleeps pleasantly,
having abandoned victory and defeat.

~ BUDDHA

SEPTEMBER 7

*To love what you do and feel
that it matters—how could
anything be more fun?*

~ KATHARINE GRAHAM

*Be grateful for luck. Pay the thunder no mind.
Listen to the birds. And don't hate nobody.*

-- JAMES HUBERT "EUBIE" BLAKE

SEPTEMBER 9

*When you come right down to it,
the secret of having it all is loving it all.*

~ JOYCE BROTHERS

A bed, a nice fresh bed, with smoothly drawn sheets and a hot-water bottle at the end of it, soft to the feet like a live animal's tummy.

~ COLETTE

A woman is never sexier than when she's comfortable in her clothes.

~ VERA WANG

*Go outside and try to
recapture the happiness
within yourself;
think of all the beauty
in yourself and in
everything around you
and be happy.*

~ ANNE FRANK

SEPTEMBER 13

The ideal of calm exists in a sitting cat.

~ JULES RENARD

Anyone's life truly lived consists
of work, sunshine, exercise,
soap, plenty of fresh air,
and a happy contented spirit.

~ Lillie Langtry

The greater part of our happiness or misery depends on our dispositions, and not upon our circumstances.

~ MARTHA WASHINGTON

I never found the companion that was
so companionable as solitude.

~ HENRY DAVID THOREAU

SEPTEMBER 17

*I have perceived that
to be with those I like
is enough.*

~ WALT WHITMAN

SEPTEMBER 18

We are happy when
we are growing.

~ W. B. YEATS

If you are lonely when you're alone,
you are in bad company.

~ JEAN-PAUL SARTRE

SEPTEMBER 20

Be content with what you have;
rejoice in the way things are.
When you realize there is nothing lacking,
the whole world belongs to you.

~ LAO-TZU

Taking a midday nap
feet planted
on a cool wall.

~ MATSUO BASHŌ

A book of verses underneath the bough,
A jug of wine, a loaf of bread, and thou
Beside me singing in the wilderness—
Oh, wilderness is paradise now.

~ OMAR KHAYYÁM

SEPTEMBER 23

*Never look at what
you have lost;
look at what you
have left.*

~ ROBERT H. SCHULLER

SEPTEMBER 24

*If you can't do great
things yourself, remember
that you may do small
things in a great way.*

~ NAPOLEON HILL

*It is with life as it is with a play—
it matters not how long the action is
spun out, but how good the acting is.*

~ LUCIUS ANNAEUS SENECA

You will never be able to escape from your heart. So it's better to listen to what it has to say.

~ PAULO COELHO

One joy scatters a hundred griefs.

~ CHINESE PROVERB

SEPTEMBER 28

*The butterfly counts not months
but moments, and has time enough.*

~ RABINDRANATH TAGORE

SEPTEMBER 29

*It is neither wealth nor splendor,
but tranquility and occupation,
which give happiness.*

~ THOMAS JEFFERSON

The foolish man seeks happiness in the distance;
the wise grows it under his own feet.

~ JAMES OPPENHEIM

OCTOBER

WISDOM

One must view the world through the eye in one's heart rather than just trust the eyes in one's head.

~ MARY CROW DOG

OCTOBER 2

What are heavy? Sea-sand and sorrow;
What are brief? Today and tomorrow;
What are frail? Spring blossoms and youth;
What are deep? The ocean and truth.

~ CHRISTINA ROSSETTI

OCTOBER 3

Fall seven times, stand up eight.

~ JAPANESE PROVERB

Think before you speak.
Read before you think.

~ FRAN LEBOWITZ

OCTOBER 5

Fate keeps on happening.

~ ANITA LOOS

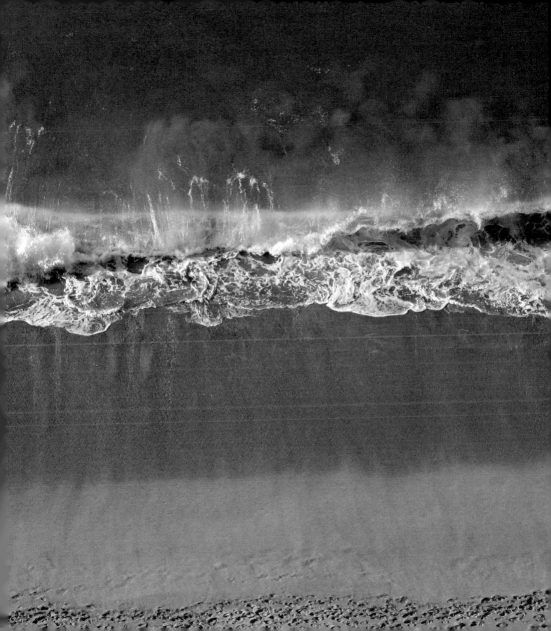

OCTOBER 6

The present was an egg
laid by the past that had the future
inside its shell.

~ ZORA NEALE HURSTON

OCTOBER 7

*Be more concerned with your character
than your reputation.*

~ JOHN WOODEN

Don't compromise yourself.
You are all you've got.

~ JANIS JOPLIN

It is hard to fight an enemy who has outposts in your head.

~ SALLY KEMPTON

A thousand words leave not
the same deep print as does a single deed.

~ HENRIK IBSEN

OCTOBER 11

*It's more fun to be a pirate
than to join the navy.*

STEVE JOBS

OCTOBER 12

Cease to be a drudge;
seek to be an artist.

~ MARY MCLEOD BETHUNE

OCTOBER 13

By three methods we may learn wisdom:
First, by reflection, which is noblest;
second, by imitation, which is easiest;
and third by experience,
which is the bitterest.

~ CONFUCIUS

OCTOBER 14

I don't believe that life is supposed to make you feel good, or to make you feel miserable either. Life is just supposed to make you feel.

~ GLORIA NAYLOR

Surviving is important,
but thriving is elegant.

~ MAYA ANGELOU

Long experience has taught me that to be criticized is not always to be wrong.

~ ANTHONY EDEN

*Change will only come about when we become
more forgiving, compassionate, loving, and above
all joyful in the knowledge that we can change as
those around us can change too.*

~ MAIREAD MAGUIRE

Science is not only compatible with spirituality; it is a profound source of spirituality.

~ CARL SAGAN

But one does not forget by trying to forget.
One only remembers.

~ RICHARD RODRIGUEZ

*The sea does not reward those who are
too anxious, too greedy, or too impatient.
One should lie empty, open, choiceless as a beach—
waiting for a gift from the sea.*

~ ANNE MORROW LINDBERGH

There are two ways of getting home.
One of them is to stay there;
the other is to walk round the whole
world till we come back to the same place.

~ G. K. CHESTERTON

OCTOBER 22

Look twice before you leap.

~ CHARLOTTE BRONTË

Our children may learn about
the heroes of the past. Our task is to make
ourselves the architects of the future.

~ JOMO KENYATTA

You may have noticed that if one has money
without brains, he cannot use it to advantage;
but if one has brains without money, they will enable
him to live comfortably to the end of his days.

~ L. FRANK BAUM

October 25

You can't be brave if you've only had wonderful things happen to you.

~ MARY TYLER MOORE

Trouble is part of your life.
If you don't share it, you don't give
the person who loves you a
chance to love you enough.

~ DINAH SHORE

*The first thing to do is fall in love
with your work.*

~ PROVERB

OCTOBER 28

Some things arrive on their own mysterious hour — on their own terms and not yours — to be seized or relinquished forever.

~ GAIL GODWIN

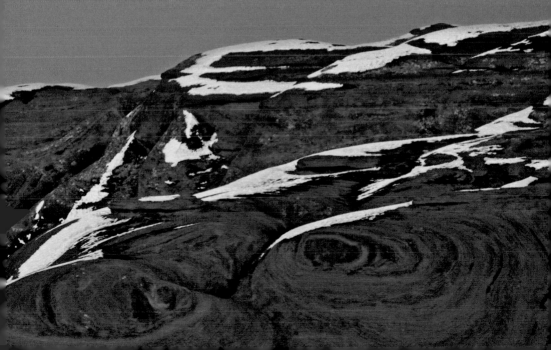

OCTOBER 29

If you rest, you rust.

~ HELEN HAYES

The secret of life and art is the threefold:
getting started, keeping going,
and getting started again.

~ SEAMUS HEANEY

OCTOBER 31

*Knowledge does not come
to us by details, but in
flashes of light from heaven.*

~ HENRY DAVID THOREAU

NOVEMBER

GRATITUDE

NOVEMBER 1

Blessings flow in the space
of gratitude.

~ OPRAH WINFREY

November 2

We should not spoil what we have by
desiring what we do not have,
but remember that what we have too was
the gift of fortune.

~ Epicurus

Everything has its beauty,
but not everyone sees it.

~ CONFUCIUS

NOVEMBER 4

Reflect on our present blessings
of which every man has many—
not on your past misfortunes,
of which all men have some.

~ CHARLES DICKENS

*Silent gratitude isn't very much
to anyone.*

~ GERTRUDE STEIN

November 6

*Walk as if you were kissing
the earth with your feet.*

~ Thich Nhat Hanh

As we express our gratitude,
we must never forget that the highest
appreciation is not to utter words,
but to live by them.

~ JOHN F. KENNEDY

NOVEMBER 8

We can only be said to be alive in
those moments when our hearts are
conscious of our treasures.

~ THORNTON WILDER

Happiness doesn't come as a result of getting something we don't have, but of recognizing and appreciating what we do have.

~ FREDERICK KOENIG

*I would maintain that thanks are the highest
form of thought; and that gratitude is
happiness doubled by wonder.*

~ G. K. CHESTERTON

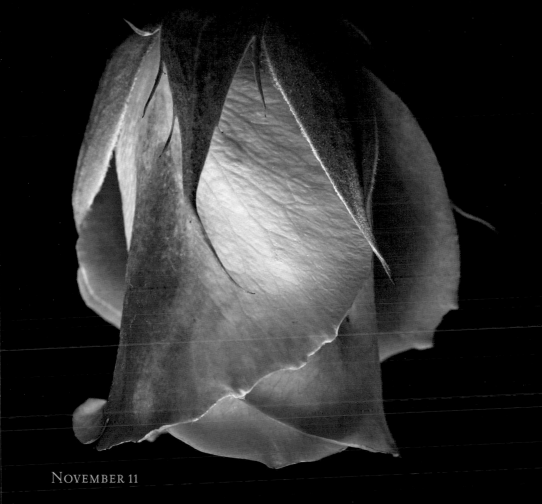

NOVEMBER 11

Some people are always grumbling because roses have thorns; I am grateful that thorns have roses.

~ JEAN-BAPTISTE ALPHONSE KARR

NOVEMBER 12

He is richest
who is content
with least.

~ SOCRATES

*It's in the human spirit
to remember a giving hand.*

~ AUDREY HEPBURN

NOVEMBER 14

*Take as a gift whatever
the day brings forth.*

~ HORACE

NOVEMBER 15

Rest and be thankful.

~ WILLIAM WORDSWORTH

*When we lose one blessing, another is often
most unexpectedly given in its place.*

~ C. S. LEWIS

NOVEMBER 17

*Every hour of the light
and dark is a miracle.*

~ WALT WHITMAN

*Watch the stars, and see yourself
running with them.*

~ MARCUS AURELIUS

NOVEMBER 19

Appreciation is a wonderful thing. It makes what is excellent in others belong to us as well.

~ VOLTAIRE

NOVEMBER 20

*If more of us valued food and cheer
and song above hoarded gold,
it would be a merrier world.*

~ J. R. R. TOLKIEN

NOVEMBER 21

The thankful receiver
bears a plentiful harvest.

~ WILLIAM BLAKE

*Wake at dawn with winged heart and
give thanks for another day of loving.*

~ KAHLIL GIBRAN

It was only a sunny smile,
and little it cost in the giving;
but it scattered the night
Like morning light,
And made the day worth living.

~ TRADITIONAL AMERICAN POEM

NOVEMBER 24

When you drink the water,
remember the well.

~ CHINESE PROVERB

The critical thing is whether you take things for granted or take them with gratitude.

~ G. K. CHESTERTON

NOVEMBER 26

There are times when we stop. We sit still . . .
We listen and breezes from a whole other world
begin to whisper.

~ JAMES CARROLL

*Gratitude is the memory
of the heart.*

~ JEAN BAPTISTE MASSIEU

NOVEMBER 28

Thankfulness is the tune of angels.

~ EDMUND SPENSER

Happiness is a butterfly, which, when pursued,
is always just beyond your grasp,
but which, if you will sit down quietly,
may alight upon you.

~ AMERICAN PROVERB

*The grateful heart sits at
a continuous feast.*

~ PROVERBS 15:15

DECEMBER

SERENITY

DECEMBER 1

*Our work for peace must begin
within the private world
of each one of us.*

~ DAG HAMMARSKJÖLD

DECEMBER 2

*Each dream finds a shape in the end;
there is a draught to quench every thirst,
and a love for every heart.*

~ GUSTAVE FLAUBERT

It isn't enough to talk about peace;
one must believe in it.
And it isn't enough to believe in it;
one must work at it.

- ELEANOR ROOSEVELT

*To sit with a dog on a hillside
on a glorious afternoon
is to be back in Eden,
where doing nothing was
not boring. It was peace.*

~ MILAN KUNDERA

DECEMBER 5

The sea
Something to look at
When we are angry.

~ UNKNOWN JAPANESE POET

DECEMBER 6

Climb the mountains and get their good tidings. Nature's peace will flow into you as sunshine flows into trees.

~ JOHN MUIR

Now stir the fire, and close the shutters fast
Let fall the curtains, wheel the sofa round . . .
So let us welcome peaceful evening in.

~ WILLIAM COWPER

Water becomes clear through stillness.
How can I become still?
By flowing with the stream.

~ LAO-TZU

DECEMBER 9

The house was quiet and the world was calm.
The reader became the book.

~ WALLACE STEVENS

DECEMBER 10

I rest in the grace of the world,
and am free.

~ WENDELL BERRY

DECEMBER 11

Blue evening falls,
Blue evening falls;
Nearby in every direction,
It sets the corn tassels trembling.

~ PAPAGO INDIAN SONG

DECEMBER 12

*However vast the darkness,
we must supply our own light.*

~ STANLEY KUBRICK

DECEMBER 13

*Courage is the price
that life extracts
for granting peace.*

~ AMELIA EARHART

*I do not at all understand the mystery of grace—
only that it meets us where we are but does not
leave us where it found us.*

~ ANNE LAMOTT

*Only the development of compassion
and understanding for others can bring us the
tranquility and happiness we all seek.*

~ DALAI LAMA

DECEMBER 16

Peace is not the absence of conflict,
but the ability to cope with conflict
by peaceful means.

- RONALD REAGAN

DECEMBER 17

*He has great tranquility of heart
who cares for neither
praise nor blame.*

~ THOMAS À KEMPIS

A mistake in judgment isn't fatal,
but too much anxiety
about judgment is.

~ PAULINE KAEL

DECEMBER 19

*Deep breaths are very helpful
at shallow parties.*

~ BARBARA WALTERS

*Your mind will answer most
questions if you learn to relax
and wait for the answer.*

~ WILLIAM S. BURROUGHS

Stress cannot exist in the presence of a pie.

~ DAVID MAMET

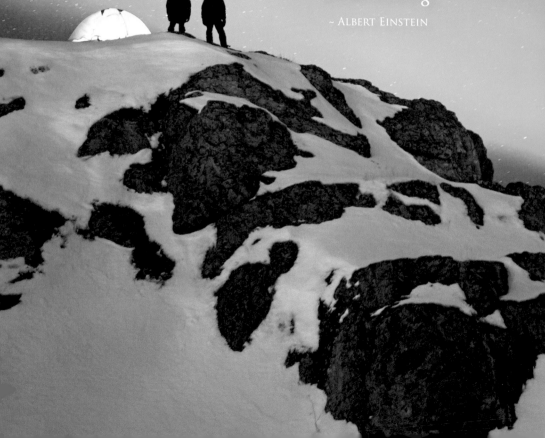

Peace cannot be kept by force;
it can only be achieved by
understanding.

~ ALBERT EINSTEIN

DECEMBER 23

Go within every day and find the inner
strength so that the world will not blow
your candle out.

~ KATHERINE DUNHAM

DECEMBER 24

To have darkness behind me,
in front of me a bright sky, flickering lights
on the water, and to feel
on the stony face the southern sun.

~ JULIA HARTWIG

DECEMBER 25

We place a happy life in a tranquility of mind.

~ CICERO

There is no way to peace;
peace is the way.

~ MAHATMA GANDHI

Do your work, then step back.
The only path to serenity.

~ LAO-TZU

DECEMBER 28

Better than a thousand
hollow words is one word
that brings peace.

~ BUDDHA

*None but ourselves
can free our minds.*

~ BOB MARLEY

Far from idleness being the root of all evil,
it is rather the only true good.

~ SØREN KIERKEGAARD

DECEMBER 31

Either peace or happiness,
let it enfold you.

~ CHARLES BUKOWSKI

CREDITS

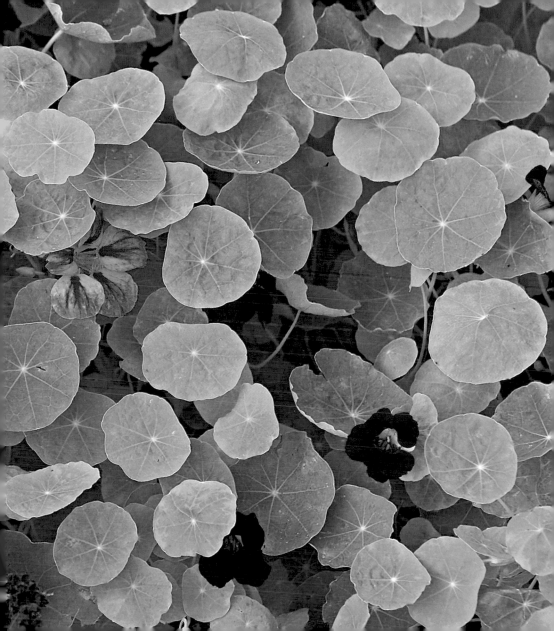

CONTRIBUTOR INDEX

Buffett, Warren
b. 1930
American investor and
philanthropist.

Bukowski, Charles
1920–1994
German-American poet,
novelist, and short-story
writer.

Burroughs, John
1837–1921
American naturalist and
essayist.

Burroughs, William
Seward
1914–1997
American author.

Burstyn, Ellen
b. 1932
American actress.

C
Campbell, Joseph John
1904–1987
American mythologist,
writer, and lecturer

Capote, Truman
1924–1984
American author.

Carroll, James
b. 1943
American journalist,
historian, and author.

Carson, Rachel
1907–1964
American marine biologist,
writer, and conservationist.

Cather, Willa
1873–1947
American author.

Cervantes Saavedra,
Miguel de
1547–1616
Spanish novelist,
playwright, and poet.

Chanel, Coco (Gabrielle)
1883–1971
French fashion designer.

Chesterton, G. K. (Gilbert
Keith)
1874–1936
British journalist,
playwright, philosopher,
poet, and critic.

Child, Julia
1912–2004
American chef and
cookbook author.

Chödrön, Pema (Deirdre
Blomfield-Brown)
b. 1936
American teacher, author,
and Tibetan Buddhist nun.

Churchill, Winston Spencer
1874–1965
British prime minister and
statesman.

Cicero, Marcus Tullius
106–43 B.C.
Roman philosopher,
statesman, and orator.

Coelho, Paulo
b. 1947

Brazilian novelist and
lyricist.

Colette (Sidonie-
Gabrielle)
1873–1954
French novelist.

Confucius
551–479 B.C.
Chinese philosopher and
teacher.

Cousteau, Jacques-Yves
1910–1997
French author and
oceanographer.

Cowper, William
1731–1800
English poet and
hymnodist.

Crow Dog, Mary
1954–2013
Sicangu Lakota writer and
activist.

Cunningham, Evelyn
1916–2010
American journalist.

D
Dalai Lama (Tenzin
Gyatso)
b. 1935
Tibetan spiritual and
political leader.

Dickens, Charles
1812–1870
English writer and social
critic.

Didion, Joan
b. 1934
American journalist and
novelist.

Dillard, Annie
b. 1945
American poet, essayist,
and literary critic.

Disraeli, Benjamin
1804–1881
British prime minister.

Douglass, Frederick
1818–1895
American social reformer,
writer, and orator.

Dumas, Alexandre
1802–1870
French playwright,
historian, and author.

Dunham, Katherine
1909–2006
American dancer, social
activist, and author.

Dürer, Albrecht
1471–1528
German painter,
mathematician, and
theorist.

E
Earhart, Amelia
1897–1937
American aviator.

Ebner-Eschenbach,
Marie von
1830–1916
Austrian writer.

Edelman, Marian Wright
b. 1939
American activist.

Eden, Anthony
1897–1977
British prime minister.

Einstein, Albert
1879–1955
German-American
theoretical physicist.

Eliot, George (Mary Ann
Evans)
1819–1880
British novelist.

Eliot, T. S. (Thomas
Stearns)
1888–1965
British poet and playwright.

Ellington, Duke (Edward
Kennedy)
1899-1974
American composer,
pianist, and big-band
leader.

Ellison, Ralph
1914–1994
American novelist and
scholar.

Emerson, Ralph Waldo
1803–1882
American essayist, lecturer,
and poet.

Ephron, Nora
1941–2012
American screenwriter,
director, and journalist.

Epictetus
A.D. 55–135
Greek sage and Stoic
philosopher.

Epicurus
341–269 B.C.
Greek philosopher.

F
Fisher, M. F. K. (Mary
Frances Kennedy)
1908–1992
American food writer.

Flaubert, Gustave
1821–1880
French novelist.

Fonteyn, Margot
1919–1991
English ballerina.

Forbes, Malcolm
1919–1990
American businessman
and publisher.

Frank, Anne
1929–1945
German diarist.

Franklin, Benjamin
1706–1790
American inventor, author,
politician, diplomat, and
scientist.

Friedman, Bonnie
b. 1958
American author.

Frost, Robert
1874–1963

American poet.

G
Gandhi, Mohandas
Karamchand (Mahatma)
1869–1948
Indian civil rights leader.

Gibran, Kahlil
1883–1931
Lebanese-American
artist, poet, writer, and
philosopher.

Gide, André Paul
Guillaume
1869–1947
French author.

Ginsburg, Ruth Bader
b. 1933
Associate justice of the
U.S. Supreme Court.

Giovanni, Nikki (Yolande
Cornelia)
b. 1943
American poet.

Glass, Philip
b. 1937
American composer.

Godwin, Gail
b. 1937
American novelist and
short-story writer.

Goethe, Johann Wolfgang von
1749–1832
German novelist,
poet, playwright, and
philosopher.

Gogh, Vincent Willem van
1853–1890
Dutch painter.

Goldsmith, Joan Oliver
b. 1951
American author,
singer, and professional
speaker.

Goodall, Jane
b. 1934
British primatologist and
anthropologist.

Graham, Katharine
1917–2001
American publisher.

Greer, Germaine
b. 1939
Australian journalist and
academic.

H
Hammarskjöld, Dag
1905–1961
Swedish diplomat,
economist, and author.

Hanh, Thich Nhat
b. 1926
Vietnamese Buddhist
monk, poet, author, and
activist.

Hartwig, Julia
b. 1921
Polish poet.

Hayes, Helen
1900–1993
American actress.

Heaney, Seamus
b. 1939
Irish poet.

Hepburn, Audrey
1929–1993
British actress and
humanitarian.

Hesse, Hermann
1877–1962
German-Swiss poet,
novelist, and painter.

Hill, Napoleon
1883–1970
American author, lawyer,
and journalist.

Hillesum, Etty (Esther)
1914–1943
Dutch-Jewish writer.

Holmes, Oliver Wendell,
Sr.
1809–1894
American physician,
professor, and author.

Horace (Quintus Horatius
Flaccus)
65–27 B.C.
Roman lyric poet.

Hugo, Victor
1802–1885
French poet, novelist, and
dramatist.

Hurston, Zora Neale
1891–1960
American novelist, essayist,
and folklorist.

I

Ibsen, Henrik
1828–1906
Norwegian playwright and
poet.

Ingersoll, Robert Green
1833–1899
American politician and
orator.

Irving, Washington
1783–1859
American author, essayist,
biographer, and historian.

J

Jefferson, Thomas
1743–1826
American President.

Jin, Ha (Jīn Xuéfēi)
b. 1956
Chinese-American writer
and novelist.

Jobs, Steve
1955–2011
American businessman,
innovator, and
entrepreneur.

Joplin, Janis
1943–1970
American singer-
songwriter.

Joyce, James
1882–1941
Irish novelist and poet.

Jung, Carl (Gustav)
1875–1961
Swiss psychiatrist and

founder of analytical
psychology.

K

Kael, Pauline
1919–2001
American film critic.

Kafka, Franz
1883–1924
Austro-Hungarian novelist.

Karr, Jean-Baptiste
Alphonse
1808–1890
French journalist, critic,
and novelist.

Keats, John
1795–1821
British poet.

Keen, Sam
b. 1931
American author,
philosopher, and professor.

Keller, Helen
1880–1968
American writer, lecturer,
and activist.

Kempton, Sally
American spiritual teacher
and author.

Kennedy, John Fitzgerald
1917–1963
American President.

Kenyatta, Jomo
1893–1978
Kenyan prime minister
and president.

Khayyám, Omar
1048–1131
Persian philosopher,
astronomer, and poet.

Kierkegaard, Søren
1813–1855
Danish philosopher,
theologian, and writer.

King, Martin Luther, Jr.
1929–1968
American clergyman,
activist, and leader.

Kingsolver, Barbara
b. 1955
American novelist, poet,
and essayist.

Koenig, Friedrich
1774–1833
German inventor.

Kubrick, Stanley
1928–1999
American film
director, producer,
and screenwriter.

Kundera, Milan
b. 1929
Czech writer.

L

Lamott, Anne
b. 1954
American novelist and
nonfiction writer.

L'Amour, Louis
1908–1988
American author.

Langtry, Lillie
1853–1929
British singer and actress.

Lao-tzu
604–531 B.C.
Chinese philosopher.

Lebowitz, Fran
b. 1950
American author.

Leclerc de Buffon,
Georges-Louis
1707–1788
French naturalist,
cosmologist, and author.

Le Guin, Ursula K.
b. 1929
American novelist, poet,
and essayist.

L'Engle, Madeleine
1918–2007
American novelist.

Leonardo da Vinci
1452–1519
Italian artist, inventor,
and writer.

Lewis, C. S. (Clive
Staples)
1898–1963
Irish novelist, scholar, and
broadcaster.

Lincoln, Abraham
1809–1865
American President.

Lindbergh, Anne Morrow
1906–2001

American writer, poet,
and aviator.

Lin Yutang
1895–1976
Chinese novelist, essayist,
and translator.

Little, Mary Wilson
American writer.

Longfellow, Henry
Wadsworth
1807–1882
American poet.

Loos, Anita
1889–1981
American screenwriter,
playwright, and author.

Loren, Sophia
b. 1934
Italian actress.

Luther, Martin
1483–1546
German monk, priest, and
professor.

M
Maguire, Mairead
b. 1944
Northern Irish peace
activist.

Mamet, David
b. 1947
American playwright,
essayist, and film director.

Mann, Thomas
1875–1955
German novelist.

Mansfield, Katherine
1888–1923
New Zealand–born
modernist writer.

Marcus Aurelius
A.D. 121–180
Roman emperor.

Marley, Bob (Nesta
Robert)
1945–1981
Jamaican singer-
songwriter and musician.

Massieu, Jean Baptiste
1772–1846
French educator.

McCandless, Christopher
Johnson (Alexander
Supertramp)
1968–1992
American adventurer.

McCarthy, Mary
1912–1989
American author.

McLaughlin, Mignon
1913–1983
American journalist and
writer.

Mead, Margaret
1901–1978
American cultural
anthropologist.

Merton, Thomas
1915–1968
American writer.

Miller, Henry

1891–1980
American novelist.

Milne, A. A. (Alan
Alexander)
1882–1956
English novelist, poet, and
playwright.

Milton, John
1608–1674
English poet and civil
servant.

Mingus, Charles
1922–1979
American composer,
bassist, and bandleader.

Molière (Jean-Baptiste
Poquelin)
1622–1673
French playwright and
actor.

Montaigne, Michel de
1533–1592
French writer and
philosopher.

Moore, Mary Tyler
b. 1936
American actress.

Morris, William
1834–1896
English artist, writer, and
designer.

al-Muhasibi, al-Harith
781–857
Theologian and Sufi
teacher.

Muir, John
1838–1914
Scottish-American
naturalist, author, and
activist.

Mumford, Lewis
1895–1990
American historian,
philosopher, and literary
critic.

Murdoch, Iris
1919–1999
British novelist and
philosopher.

N
Nabokov, Vladimir
1899–1977
Russian-American novelist.

Naylor, Gloria
b. 1950
African-American
novelist and educator.

Nietzsche, Friedrich
1844–1900
German philosopher and
poet.

Nin, Anaïs
1903–1977
French diarist and novelist.

Norris, Kathleen
b. 1947
American poet and
essayist.

O
Obama, Michelle
b. 1964

American First Lady,
lawyer, and activist.

Oppenheim, James
1882–1932
American poet, novelist,
and editor.

Osho (Bhagwan Shree
Rajneesh)
1931–1990
Indian mystic, guru, and
spiritual teacher.

Ozick, Cynthia
b. 1928
American novelist and
essayist.

P
Penn, William
1644–1718
English philosopher.

Picasso, Pablo
1881–1973
Spanish artist.

Plath, Sylvia
1932–1963
American poet, novelist,
and short-story writer.

Pollan, Michael
b. 1955
American journalist,
author, and professor.

Porter, Katherine Anne
1890–1980
American journalist,
novelist, and political
activist.

Proust, Marcel
1871–1922
French novelist.

Q
Quindlen, Anna
b. 1953
American journalist and
novelist.

R
Ramakrishna, Sri
1836–1886
Indian priest and spiritual
leader.

Reagan, Ronald
1911–2004
American President and
actor.

Renard, Jules
1864–1910
French author.

Reynolds, Sir Joshua
1723–1792
English painter.

Rich, Adrienne
1929–2012
American poet, essayist,
and feminist.

Robinson, Marilynne
b. 1943
American novelist and
essayist.

Rodriguez, Richard
b. 1944
American writer.

Rogers, Ginger (Virginia

Katherine McMath)
1911–1995
American actress, dancer,
and singer.

Roosevelt, (Anna) Eleanor
1884–1962
American First Lady,
activist, and author.

Roosevelt, Theodore
1858–1919
American President.

Rossetti, Christina
1830–1894
English poet.

Rousseau, Jean-Jacques
1712–1778
Swiss philosopher and
writer.

Rukeyser, Muriel
1913–1980
American poet and
political activist.

Rumi (Jalal ad-Din
ar-Rumi)
1207–1273
Persian poet.

Russell, Bertrand
1872–1970
British philosopher,
mathematician, and social
critic.

S
Sagan, Carl
1934–1996
American astronomer,
astrophysicist, and author.

Sand, George
(Amandine-Aurore-
Lucile Dupin)
1804–1876
French novelist and
memoirist.

Santayana, George
1863–1952
Spanish-American
philosopher, poet, and
novelist.

Sarton, May (Eleanore
Marie)
1912–1995
American poet, novelist,
and memoirist.

Sartre, Jean-Paul
1905–1980
French philosopher,
playwright, and novelist.

Savage, Minot Judson
1841–1918
American minister and
author.

Schuller, Robert Harold
b. 1926
American televangelist
and author.

Schulz, Charles Monroe
1922–2000
American cartoonist.

Schweitzer, Albert
1875–1965
German and French
philosopher, musician,
and physician.

Seeger, Pete
b. 1919
American folk singer.

Seneca, Lucius Annaeus
(Seneca the Younger)
4 B.C.–A.D. 65
Roman philosopher,
statesman, and
dramatist.

Shakespeare, William
1564–1616
British playwright and
poet.

Shaw, George Bernard
1856–1950
Irish playwright.

Sheehy, Gail
b. 1937
American journalist and
author.

Shore, Dinah
1916–1994
American singer and
actress.

Shushiki, Ome
1668–1725
Japanese poet.

Socrates
469–399 B.C.
Greek philosopher.

Spencer, Diana
1961–1997
Wife of Charles, Prince of
Wales, and international
humanitarian.

Spenser, Edmund
1552–1599
English poet.

Stein, Gertrude
1874–1946
American novelist and
poet.

Stevens, Wallace
1879–1955
American Modernist
poet.

Strunk, William, Jr.
1869–1946
American author and
professor.

Szymborska, Wisława
1923–2012
Polish poet and essayist.

T
Tagore, Rabindranath
1861–1941
Bengali poet, novelist,
essayist, and composer.

Teale, Edwin Way
1899–1980
American naturalist,
writer, and photographer.

Teresa, Mother (Agnes
Gonxha Bojaxhiu)
1910–1997
Albanian-Indian nun and
religious leader.

Thomas à Kempis
1380–1471
Dutch priest, monk, and
writer.

Thoreau, Henry David
1817–1862
American author, poet,
and philosopher.

Thurber, James
1894–1961
American cartoonist and
humorist.

Tolkien, J. R. R. (John
Ronald Reuel)
1892–1973
English writer, poet, and
professor.

Tolstoy, Leo
1828–1910
Russian novelist and
short-story writer.

Tutu, Desmond
b. 1931
South African religious
leader and antiapartheid
activist.

Twain, Mark (Samuel
Langhorne Clemens)
1835–1910
American novelist and
humorist.

U
Updike, John
1932–2009
American novelist, poet,
and critic.

V
Vivekananda, Swami
(Narendra Nath Datta)
1863–1902
Indian Hindu monk.

Voltaire (François-Marie Arouet)
1694–1778
French writer, playwright, and philosopher.

Vonnegut, Kurt, Jr.
1922–2007
American writer.

W

Walker, Alice
b. 1944
American novelist, poet, and activist.

Walters, Barbara
b. 1929
American journalist, author, and media personality.

Wang, Vera
b. 1949
American fashion designer.

Washington, George
1732–1799
American President.

Washington, Martha
1731–1802
American First Lady.

Waters, Alice
b. 1944
American chef, activist, and author.

Weil, Simone
1909–1943
French philosopher and social activist.

West, Mae (Mary Jane)
1893–1980
American actress, playwright, and screenwriter.

Westheimer, Ruth
b. 1928
American media personality.

White, E. B. (Elwyn Brooks)
1899–1985
American writer.

Whitman, Walt
1819–1892
American poet, essayist, and journalist.

Whittier, John Greenleaf
1807–1892
American Quaker poet.

Wilde, Oscar
1854–1900
Irish novelist and dramatist.

Wilder, Laura Ingalls
1867–1957
American author.

Wilder, Thornton
1897–1975
American playwright and novelist.

Williams, Tennessee (Thomas Lanier)
1911–1983
American playwright, novelist, and essayist.

Wilson, Edmund
1895–1972
American writer.

Winfrey, Oprah
b. 1954
American media personality.

Wooden, John
1910–2010
American basketball player and coach.

Woollcott, Alexander
1887–1943
American playwright and drama critic.

Wordsworth, William
1770–1850
English poet.

Wyatt, Thomas
1503–1542
English ambassador and poet.

Y

Yeats, W. B. (William Butler)
1865–1939
Irish poet

ILLUSTRATIONS CREDITS

Cover, asharkyu/Shutterstock.

Opener, Aleksandr Volkov/iStockphoto; Title Page, Ian Flindt/NG My Shot; Table of Contents, WitR/Shutterstock.

January
Opener, Faizan Khan/NG My Shot; 1, Zeng Shun/NG My Shot; 2, Alaska Stock Images/NG Stock; 3, aruru/Shutterstock; 4, IrinaK/Shutterstock; 5, Lincoln Harrison/NG My Shot; 6, Giorgio Fochesato/iStockphoto; 7, Gwoeii/Shutterstock; 8, Oliver Kennedy/NG My Shot; 9, NASA/ESA; 10, FloridaStock/Shutterstock; 11, Frans Lanting/NG Stock; 12, William Rizzoli/NG My Shot; 13, Robert Hooper/NG My Shot; 14, Michele Cox/Shutterstock; 15, Dmitri Mikitenko/Shutterstock; 16, Elenarts/iStockphoto; 17, Gabriel Carlson/NG My Shot; 18, Leigh Prather/Shutterstock; 19, JasonDoiy/iStockphoto; 20, idreamphoto/Shutterstock; 21, Veronika Kolev/NG My Shot; 22, Jodi Cobb/NG Stock; 23, Bjorn Anders Nymoen/NG My Shot; 24, Guido Mocafico; 25, Nils Z/Shutterstock; 26, Sungjin Kim/NG My Shot; 27, Juan Manuel Moreno/NG My Shot; 28, worker/Shutterstock; 29, rozbyshaka/Shutterstock; 30, Todd Keith/iStockphoto; 31, Rechitan Sorin/Shutterstock.

February
Opener, Susan Stanton/NG My Shot; 1, Anson0618/Shutterstock; 2, James P. Blair/NG Stock; 3, Jun Yan Loke/iStockphoto; 4, Hiroshi Chang/NG My Shot; 5, Galina Barskaya/Shutterstock; 6, David Alan Harvey/NG Stock; 7, Larry Paris/NG My Shot; 8, Jose Ignacio Soto/Shutterstock; 9, Autumn Schanil/NG My Shot; 10, Veniamin Kraskov/Shutterstock; 11, Jodi Cobb/NG Stock; 12, Peter Pevy/NG My Shot; 13, Mark Duffy/NG My Shot; 14, Jill Cossu/NG My Shot; 15, Rafal Olkis/Shutterstock; 16, Joel Sartore/NG Stock; 17, Pius Lee/Shutterstock; 18, Jak Wonderly/NG My Shot; 19, Marie Destefanis/NG My Shot; 20, shooarts/Shutterstock; 21, Jack Fusco/NG My Shot; 22, Zamada/Shutterstock; 23, Filip Fuxa/Shutterstock; 24, Asisthya Muluk/NG My Shot; 25, Mustafiz Mamun/NG My Shot; 26, Eduardo Jose Bernardino/iStockphoto; 27, Rechitan Sorin/Shutterstock; 28/29, Michael Nichols/NG Stock.

March
Opener, Jim Richardson/NG Stock; 1, Jan Sommer/Shutterstock; 2, Dima Sobko/Shutterstock; 3, Anna Subbotina/Shutterstock; 4, Chris Parsons/NG My Shot; 5, desuza.communications/iStockphoto; 6, Johan Swanepoel/Shutterstock; 7, Marie C. Fields/Shutterstock; 8, Oleg Zhukov/Shutterstock; 9, bjdlzx/iStockphoto; 10, Darlyne A. Murawski/NG Stock; 11, Julie Shaw/NG My Shot; 12, Brad Goldpaint/NG My Shot; 13, Joseph H. Bailey/NG Stock; 14, ittipon/Shutterstock; 15, Mark Thiessen, NGS; 16, Zack Clothier/NG My Shot; 17, Jens Ottoson/Shutterstock; 18, Xiaomei Sun/NG My Shot; 19, Jim Richardson/NG Stock; 20, NG Photographer/NG Stock; 21, Michael Yamashita/NG Image Collection; 22, Pakhnyushcha/Shutterstock; 23, Roy De Haas/NG My Shot; 24, Alankar Chandra/NG My Shot; 25, Priyam Dhar/NG My Shot; 26, Nattika/Shutterstock; 27, AJ Wilhelm/NG Stock; 28, Greg Dale/NG Stock; 29, Kani Polat/NG My Shot; 30, David S. Boyer/NG Stock; 31, Greg Stafford/NG My Shot.

April
Opener, Loreto Pintado/NG My Shot; 1, Matauw/iStockphoto; 2, Sergiy Telesh/Shutterstock; 3, Rebecca Hale, NGS; 4, Egor Mopanko/iStockphoto; 5, cao yu/iStockphoto; 6, Bruce Dale/NG Stock; 7, Luther Bailey/NG My Shot; 8, Sam Abell/NG Stock; 9, Daniel Etzold/Shutterstock; 10, Stephen Strathdee/iStockphoto; 11, PuiYuen Ng/iStockphoto; 12, Irina Mosina/Shutterstock; 13, Aimin Tang/iStockphoto; 14, Sam Abell/NG Stock; 15, deb22/Shutterstock; 16, ZouZou/Shutterstock; 17, Frans Lanting/NG Stock; 18, Borut Trdina/iStockphoto; 19, Penny De Los Santos; 20, Sandra Cunningham/Shutterstock; 21, Chepe Nicoli/Shutterstock; 22, Stacy Funderburke/

NG My Shot; 23, spirit of america/Shutterstock; 24, Travis Dove/NG Stock; 25, Helene Schmitz; 26, Deron Verbeck/NG My Shot; 27, John Burcham/NG Stock; 28, technotr/iStockphoto; 29, Yongyut Kumsri/NG My Shot; 30, Rick Wianecki/NG My Shot.

May

Opener, Jim Richardson/NG Stock; 1, Joan Vicent Cantó Roig/iStockphoto; 2, Chris Hill/NG Stock; 3, George Steinmetz/NG Image Collection; 4, Emory Kristof/NG Stock; 5, Kevin Byrne/NG My Shot; 6, Olga Vasilkova/Shutterstock; 7, Veronique Fleury/NG My Shot; 8, Steve McCurry/NG Image Collection; 9, Rob Macaulay/NG My Shot; 10, Sergieiev/Shutterstock; 11, Piotr Gatlik/Shutterstock; 12, Peter Essick/NG Image Collection; 13, Josh Exell/NG My Shot; 14, blueeyes/Shutterstock; 15, Dan Lee/Shutterstock; 16, Dori O'Connell/iStockphoto; 17, Robert F. Sisson/NG Stock; 18, Helminadia Caryati/NG My Shot; 19, Josef Muellek/Shutterstock; 20, James L. Amos/NG Stock; 21, Joe Stroud/NG My Shot; 22, Alessandro Zocc/Shutterstock; 23, Nikola Spasenoski/iStockphoto; 24, Stefan Geyer/NG My Shot; 25, Chantal de Bruijne/Shutterstock; 26, Guillermo Ossa/NG My Shot; 27, Vladimir Piskunov/iStockphoto; 28, Kevin O'Brien/NG My Shot; 29, George Steinmetz/NG Stock; 30, Alan Di Lucca/NG My Shot; 31, Jodi Cobb/NG Stock.

June

Opener, Lourie Zipf/NG My Shot; 1, ben phillips/iStockphoto; 2, Renant Cheng/NG My Shot; 3, mycola/iStockphoto; 4, James P. Blair/NG Stock; 5, antb/Shutterstock; 6, Bill Hatcher/NG Stock; 7, Mauricio Handler/NG Stock; 8, Joel Sartore/NG Stock; 9, Daniel Schweinert/Shutterstock; 10, Oleg Tovkach/Shutterstock; 11, Mac99/iStockphoto; 12, defpicture/Shutterstock; 13, Markus Beck/iStockphoto; 14, He Qustuf/NG My Shot; 15, Lyn Gianni/iStockphoto; 16, Pelevina Ksinia/Shutterstock; 17, Sisse Brimberg/NG Stock; 18, Brenda Carson/Shutterstock; 19, Chuck Lund/NG Stock; 20, mypokcik/Shutterstock; 21, Mariano Fernandez/NG My Shot; 22, Greg Dale/NG Stock; 23, Andrea Haase/iStockphoto; 24, Simon Zenger/Shutterstock; 25, Lynn Johnson/NG Stock; 26, Michele Stanzione/NG My Shot; 27, Isaac Montealegre/NG My Shot; 28, peter zelei/iStockphoto; 29, Jennifer Lange/NG My Shot; 30, agcuesta/iStockphoto.

July

Opener, Nicoleta Gabor/NG My Shot; 1, Ira Block/NG Stock; 2, Marion Fauchart/NG My Shot; 3, Sisse Brimberg/NG Stock; 4, bmnarak/Shutterstock; 5, Kavin Ho/NG My Shot; 6, Jim Brandenburg/Minden Pictures/NG Stock; 7, Alaska Stock Images/NG Stock; 8, grynold/Shutterstock; 9, Ian Momsen/NG My Shot; 10, Silken Photography/Shutterstock; 11, John Seamons/NG My Shot; 12, Tim Laman/NG Stock; 13, Harry Katzjaeger/NG My Shot; 14, Kenneth Geiger, NGS; 15, Marie C. Fields/Shutterstock; 16, Angga Putra/NG My Shot; 17, Media Union/Shutterstock; 18, James L. Stanfield/NG Stock; 19, pzAxe/Shutterstock; 20, Thomas Andrijauskas/NG My Shot; 21, Janice Silvera/NG My Shot; 22, Mitsuhiko Imamori/Minden Pictures/NG Stock; 23, Rodrigo Pessoa/NG My Shot; 24, iSIRIPONG/Shutterstock; 25, Dja65/Shutterstock; 26, Colleen Pinski/NG My Shot; 27, Helene Schmitz; 28, B. Anthony Stewart/NG Stock; 29, Bhaskar Dutta/NG My Shot; 30, Xue Zehao/NG My Shot; 31, Brian A Jackson/Shutterstock.

August

Opener, Raul Touzon/NG Stock; 1, Maglara/Shutterstock; 2, saddako/Shutterstock; 3, James P. Blair/NG Stock; 4, Joe Cicak/iStockphoto; 5, Tino Soriano/NG Stock; 6, vicspacewalker/Shutterstock; 7, Julius Diaz/NG My Shot; 8, Rich Reid/NG Stock; 9, Zeeshan Butt/NG My Shot; 10, Thomas Arbour/iStockphoto; 11, rsooll/Shutterstock; 12, John Eastcott and Yva Momatiuk/NG Stock; 13, nikamata/iStockphoto; 14, kenkistler/Shutterstock; 15, Dja65/Shutterstock; 16, Todd Gipstein/NG Stock; 17, Valerie Loiseleux/iStockphoto; 18, Pete Ryan/NG Stock; 19, Bill Dalton/NG My Shot; 20, silver-john/Shutterstock; 21, David Kay/Shutterstock; 22, Lewis Tolputt/NG My Shot; 23, Joel Sartore/NG Stock; 24, Michael G. Smith/Shutterstock; 25, Joop Snijder Photography/Shutterstock; 26, Christine Kastler/NG My Shot; 27, Gordon Dixon/iStockphoto; 28, BanksPhotos/iStockphoto; 29, Paul Hayes/NG My Shot; 30, Galina Peshkova/iStockphoto; 31, Susan Law Cain/Shutterstock.

September

Opener, Alexander Ozerov/Shutterstock; 1, Taylor S. Kennedy/NG Stock; 2, Anna Subbotina/Shutterstock; 3, Sam Burt Photography/iStockphoto; 4, Konstantin

Sutyagin/iStockphoto; 5, wjarek/Shutterstock; 6, Sandra Caldwell/Shutterstock; 7, George Steinmetz/NG Stock; 8, Ray Hems/iStockphoto; 9, Keenpress/NG Stock; 10, Mike Theiss/NG Stock; 11, Abraham Nowitz/NG Stock; 12, Kanoniga Kanoniga/NG My Shot; 13, ots-photo/Shutterstock; 14, Lance Lee/iStockphoto; 15, Yevgeniy Steshkin/Shutterstock; 16, Kike Calvo/NG Stock; 17, Cyril Ruoso/JH Editorial/Minden Pictures/NG Stock; 18, Golden-Colt/iStockphoto; 19, Jitalia17/iStockphoto; 20, Julianna Olah/iStockphoto; 21, JeniFoto/Shutterstock; 22, IriskinoFoto/Shutterstock; 23, Robert F. Sisson/NG Stock; 24, Jodi Cobb/NG Stock; 25, Sailom/Shutterstock; 26, Mike Theiss/NG Stock; 27, ouh_desire/Shutterstock; 28, Dennis Tyler/NG My Shot; 29, Yves Schiepek/NG My Shot; 30, Lilli Day/iStockphoto.

October
Opener, David S. Boyer/NG Stock; 1, fstockfoto/Shutterstock; 2, Shelley Smart/NG My Shot; 3, Otis Imboden/NG Stock; 4, Ariel Batson/NG My Shot; 5, Larry Schaefer/NG My Shot; 6, Amanda Rohde/iStockphoto; 7, Lauren Geary/NG My Shot; 8, Richard T. Nowitz/NG Stock; 9, James Cumming/NG My Shot; 10, Jeremy Edwards/iStockphoto; 11, Luis Marden/NG Stock; 12, James L. Stanfield/NG Stock; 13, Kuttelvaserova Stuchelova/Shutterstock; 14, Tyrone Turner/NG Stock; 15, olivier/Shutterstock; 16, Travis Dove/NG Stock; 17, Dmitry Zimin/Shutterstock; 18, NASA, ESA, C.R. O'Dell (Vanderbilt University), M. Meixner and, P. McCullough (STScI); 19, Anna Subbotina/Shutterstock; 20, Swetlana Wall/Shutterstock; 21, Gordon (Dusty) Demerson Jr./iStockphoto; 22, Norman Setiawan/NG My Shot; 23, unknown1861/Shutterstock; 24, Michael Nichols/NG Stock; 25, Robert F. Sisson/NG Stock; 26, pakul54/Shutterstock; 27, Kenneth O'Quinn/iStockphoto; 28, Judith Zimmerman/NG My Shot; 29, Raul Touzon/NG Stock; 30, AdStock RF/Shutterstock; 31, FWStudio/Shutterstock.

November
Opener, Joel Sartore/NG Stock; 1, David Doubilet/NG Stock; 2, AMA/Shutterstock; 3, Christian Ziegler/NG Image Collection; 4, Raymond Gehman/NG Stock; 5, surasaki/Shutterstock; 6, Hnin Khine/iStockphoto; 7, Annie Griffiths/NG Stock; 8, Michael Nichols/NG Stock; 9,

Matthew Karsten/NG My Shot; 10, Vesna Sajn/iStockphoto; 11, Richard Williams/NG My Shot; 12, Alaska Stock Images/NG Stock; 13, James Pauls/iStockphoto; 14, Kelly Mader/NG My Shot; 15, Pavel L Photo and Video/Shutterstock; 16, Patricio Robles Gil/Minden Pictures/NG Stock; 17, Jan Vermeer/Minden Pictures/NG Stock; 18, Chris Johns/NG Stock; 19, Bruce Dale/NG Stock; 20, David McLain/NG Image Collection; 21, panda3800/Shutterstock; 22, David Orias/NG My Shot; 23, Peredniankina/Shutterstock; 24, Michael Yamashita/NG Stock; 25, Joseph Romeo/NG My Shot; 26, James L. Stanfield/Naitonal Geographic Stock; 27, ynamaku/iStockphoto; 28, Roxana Gonzalez/Shutterstock; 29, Ramesh Kozhissery/NG My Shot; 30, Catherine Karnow/NG Stock.

December
Opener, Hordur Finnbogason/NG My Shot; 1, Rui Saraiva/Shutterstock; 2, Rosamund Parkinson/Shutterstock; 3, Janis Litavnieks/iStockphoto; 4, Gordon Wiltsie/NG Stock; 5, Dan Desroches/NG My Shot; 6, Chris D'Ardenne/NG My Shot; 7, dotshock/Shutterstock; 8, zebra0209/Shutterstock; 9, Rick Rhay/iStockphoto; 10, Annie Griffiths/NG Stock; 11, Henryk Sadura/Shutterstock; 12, Jodi Cobb/NG Stock; 13, Jim Richardson/NG Stock; 14, Lynn Johnson/NG Stock; 15, Pagina/Shutterstock; 16, malerapaso/iStockphoto; 17, plusphoto/iStockphoto; 18, kkaplin/Shutterstock; 19, Paul Nicklen/NG Stock; 20, Andrew Klotz/NG My Shot; 21, jonathansloane/iStockphoto; 22, David Brosha/NG My Shot; 23, tazzymoto/Shutterstock; 24, Dmitry Naumov/Shutterstock; 25, OGphoto/iStockphoto; 26, Snorri Gunnarsson/NG My Shot; 27, EUROPHOTOS/Shutterstock; 28, Shawn Hughes/NG My Shot; 29, Russel Williams/iStockphoto; 30, Michelle Grenier/NG My Shot; 31, Mark Kurtz/NG My Shot.

Credits opener, mccown/Shutterstock.

Daily Calm

Published by the
National Geographic Society
John M. Fahey, *Chairman of the Board*
 and Chief Executive Officer
Declan Moore, *Executive Vice President;*
 President, Publishing and Travel
Melina Gerosa Bellows, *Executive Vice*
 President; Chief Creative Officer, Books,
 Kids, and Family

Prepared by the Book Division
Hector Sierra, *Senior Vice President*
 and General Manager
Janet Goldstein, *Senior Vice President*
 and Editorial Director
Jonathan Halling, *Design Director,*
 Books and Children's Publishing
Marianne R. Koszorus,
 Design Director, Books
Hilary Black, *Senior Editor*
R. Gary Colbert, *Production Director*
Jennifer A. Thornton,
 Director of Managing Editorial
Susan S. Blair, *Director of Photography*
Meredith C. Wilcox, *Director,*
 Administration and Rights Clearance

Staff for This Book
Anne Smyth, *Assistant Editor*
Nancy Marion, *Illustrations Editor*
Melissa Farris, *Art Director*
Shelley Sperry, *Researcher*
Marshall Kiker, *Associate Managing Editor*
Judith Klein, *Production Editor*
Lisa Walker, *Production Manager*
Katie Olsen, *Production Design Assistant*

Production Services
Phillip L. Schlosser, *Senior Vice President*
Chris Brown, *Vice President,*
 NG Book Manufacturing
George Bounelis, *Vice President,*
 Production Services
Nicole Elliott, *Manager*
Rachel Faulise, *Manager*
Robert L. Barr, *Manager*